MW00965327

Identity & Access Management (IAM) Success Tips: Volume 1

Written by Corbin H. Links, President
Links Business Group LLC

Notice: This publication is created and intended for the purpose of providing accurate information based on the real-world experience of the author and Links Business Group LLC. It is not explicitly or implicitly intended in any way to provide or render legal advice. Claims made in this publication or related advertising represent optimum cases. Buyer experience may vary.

Table of Contents

Foreword

This book is about saving time, saving money, and creating happy stakeholders. *Interested?* Then you have come to the right place! My name is Corbin Links, and I am the President of Links Business Group LLC. I also happen to be your guide on this first of many steps down the road toward a successful, fulfilling, and profitable Identity & Access Management (IAM) Program. For a snapshot of my biography, skip to page 51. But please hurry back as we have a lot of information to cover.

This book is the result of my more than 10 years experience creating, managing, implementing, and consulting in the field of Identity & Access Management – or *IAM*. Like other books in Links Business Group's *Identity Management Success* series, my goal is to simplify IAM in such a way as to make it approachable, deployable, and successful in organizations of any size or type. With that goal in mind, *IAM Success Tip, Volume 1* is the first of five books that you will need to achieve a fulfilling and successful IAM Program. Think of *Volume 1* as the first runner in a baton or relay race. *Volume 1* (mapping to IAM Stage 1 – *Concepting*) feeds *into Volume 2* (*Planning,*) *and so on through Volume 5.* A description of the *Six Stages of IAM* may be found in the *Introduction* of this book. IAM's "Sixth Stage" is labeled "Rinsing and Repeating," so there are five volumes within this series.

With this *Volume 1* book, you are presented with a rare opportunity to learn things that product vendors will not tell you, and that industry analyst firms would charge many thousands of dollars to provide just a fraction of. I transcend above the general blog squabbles, market speak, and vendor finger pointing to reveal several of IAM's key truisms. When followed exactly, and in conjunction with the other volumes in our series, *Volume 1* will pave a smooth and clear road with which to realize your strategic IAM and Business Goals.

The intended audience for this book is anyone who is involved in the Concepting, Creating, Planning, Evaluation, Implementation, and Management of IAM Projects, and software-based systems. Anyone from C-level Executives concerned with accountability issues, to Program and Project Managers tasked with large-scale IAM projects, will find something applicable in this book.

Last, but not least: *use the book*. The tips and strategies outlined in this book are intended for immediate application and implementation. I have made every effort to present the information in a usable and practical way. Links Business Group is also in the process of preparing audio versions for listeners on the go. Please check out our website at www.linksbusinessgroup.com for the latest updates. If there is another format that you would find useful, please write to Links Business Group LLC at info@linksbusinessgroup.com.

Acknowledgements

❖ First and foremost, thanks to my beloved wife Theodora Carmen Links; partner, supporter, and truly my better half for urging me to write this book and for her contributions in completing this book.

❖ All personal and company clients past and present, without whom there would be no collective experience from which to draw and share with others.

❖ The superb staff, consultants, and contractors of Links Business Group LLC.

❖ Visitors and supporters of our website, mailing list, and blog whose input I value tremendously. And of course – you the readers of this book!

All the Best, of Identity Management Success!

Corbin H. Links, President
                              Links Business Group LLC

Introduction

Identity & Access Management, or *IAM*, is by nature a vast and complex subject. Quite simply, a primary mission of this book and other materials in the Links Business Group portfolio is to break IAM down into digestible components that any organization can use to its advantage. This book also aims to transform traditional thinking about IAM with a non-traditional approach.

The reality is that *IAM is at its heart, a Business Process Management exercise, not an exercise in making vendor A's technology work with vendor B, or deploying the latest technology gizmo.* Vendor technologies and indeed the integration components of IAM garner so much attention because…..get this….. organizations – like people – want quick fixes to complex problems.

Fad Diet Programs-The Eternal Parable of Identity Management

Here is the real story. IAM –or really any Strategic Business Initiative – is often approached in a manner similar to fad dieting and fad diet programs. Here is where I like to use a personal anecdote to explain how far too many organizations view and practice IAM.

Several years ago, I had a bit of a weight problem. Nothing so significant that I couldn't get through my front door, mind you, but it was uncomfortable. I didn't even have a good excuse as some people legitimately do. The fact was, I loved food and felt powerless to stop the love. I did not either realize, or want to admit that my behavior was the cause. So, rather than address my behavior and the thought patterns that directly led to my problem, I tried fad dieting. Every time a fad diet came along, I tried it. My weight went up and down like a yo yo. I latched on to any quick fix program that came along, figuring that "this would be the one." The pill. The program. The book. Etc. The new diet program itself was going to be the solution. I wanted a program to drop the weight for me.

To make a long story short, it took several years of problem denial and a trial of every fad diet program known to man, before waking up. It's me! I'm the problem! I can't just take a pill. I have to examine the problem, determine why the problem is occurring, and then take measured strategic steps to resolve it.

Success is after all the end goal, not failure. As surely as fad diet programs do not solve the dieter's problem over time, fad IAM software tools do not solve organizational issues and challenges. What *does* work is a cohesive, strategic, focused, well-planned effort orchestrated by a good team. At Links Business Group LLC, we often share with clients up front that unless they are prepared to be successful with IAM at a full organizational level, they should consider abandoning IAM altogether.

Are there other IAM parables or metaphors you can think of? Frankenstein perhaps?

But what about the complex integration and software challenges?

To be sure, complex integration is a necessary albeit *vital* component of IAM Programs, but it comes much farther down the road. Many organizations choose to start with Integrating (IAM Stage 4,) or audit findings, or shiny new technology, and ignore (or minimize) the very things which make or break IAM Programs: *People, Requirements, and Process*. The conventional thinking is that due to the political and fiscal challenges of true IAM programs, it's less risky to focus on a tool which might – if all goes well – divert organizational/board/management attention away from the internal issues that are causing IAM to fail or to not get off the ground. I'm here to tell you that this is not the case.

If your organization already has political and fiscal challenges, then those challenges will be made ten times (or more) worse later on, if the wrong decisions are made early. If you cannot resist the temptation to look at quick fix tools, or full IAM software solutions from the outset, at least try to ignore the temptation until later IAM Stages. Success starts with IAM Stage 1 (*Concepting & Strategizing*) and this stage should be a completely tool-free, software-free discussion zone. At this stage, you should only be discussing software issues to the extent that you are defining overall strategic goals.

Additional in-depth information on this topic will be available in IAM *Success Tips: Volume 3* and *Volume 4*. Check back on our website at http://www.linksbusinessgroup.com for the latest news on the release of this volume.

Conventions used in this book

Coming from an industry that is rife with "TLA's" (Three Letter Acronyms), I will attempt to ease the situation by using these terms no more than absolutely necessary. In keeping with that rule there are just a few terms that appear often in both Links Business Group materials, and various industry sites and publications which I outline below. Understanding these terms will prove very beneficial throughout the life of your IAM Program.

❖ *IAM* is a term used throughout this book. *IAM* is a popular acronym for *Identity & Access Management*. The context here is in reference to all primary components of *IAM*, which include provisioning, access control, access methods, directory services, business process management (BPM), workflows, auditing, authorization, and reporting.

❖ *IAM Program* refers to the Project Management aspect of IAM, or *IAM managed as a Program of interrelated projects*. Unless otherwise stated, *IAM Program* refers to people, projects, project plans and strategy, *but not software*.

❖ *PRP* denotes <u>P</u>eople, <u>R</u>equirements, and <u>P</u>rocess. You will see this term appear often in Links Business Group materials. The idea is that *PRP* comes first, before vendors, tools, and analysis of your existing data and systems. Success or failure of IAM Programs *depends entirely on PRP*, and how *PRP* is implemented.

❖ *PEER* refers to <u>P</u>eace (of mind), <u>E</u>ffectiveness, <u>E</u>fficiency, and <u>R</u>e-usability. *PEER* is the "higher order state" of IAM, and the state at which Links Business Group LLC consistently strives to attain for its clients, trainees, and readers.

❖ *IPF* refers to *IAM Program Failure*. This *IPF State* is what this book – and in fact Links Business Group LLC as a company – strives to prevent in any way possible.

❖ *RIS* refers to the "Real IAM Stakeholder(s.)" These are the stakeholders that may not necessarily be the program's owners or sponsors, but have vested stakes in the successful outcome of your IAM Program.

❖ *IAM Cornerstones* refers to how Links Business Group LLC defines the three components of a full IAM implementation:

  o Access & Authorization
  o Provisioning & Management
  o Auditing & Reporting

Full implementations of multi-year IAM Programs will invariably include all three of the cornerstone components.

However, one or more of the cornerstones may not be strategically important to your organization. Please visit *Tip #6* for further information.

❖ *Identity Modeling* is the process of defining the ideal structure of an Identity for your organization, and building this structure into the directory service components of your IAM Program. Often, the ideal Identity Model *will not look anything like your current model, especially of your organization has grown significantly, has been acquired, or otherwise merged with other organizations with different models.*

→*TIP*: Identity Modeling should be a "clean slate" exercise. For more on Identity Modeling, visit our companion website at http://www.linksbusinessgroup.com/

❖ *IAM Framework* refers to the software, network, and system-based components of your overall IAM Program. The framework provides the means to integrate business processes and software applications. In general, we use the term *Framework* to refer to software/system components, and *Program* to refer to the IAM project/initiative as a whole.

❖ →*TIP: Our famous "bonus tip" convention is used throughout our books and materials to denote special supplemental information or bonus tips.*

IAM in stages

There are essentially six stages of a full IAM Program:

1. *Concepting & Strategizing*
2. *Planning & Organizing*

3. *Designing & Architecting*
4. *Implementing & Integrating*
5. *Maintaining & Supporting*
6. *Rinsing & Repeating*

Viewed another way, it all comes down to a modified Software Development Life Cycle, or *SDLC*. Not to get on the subject of various development models, which could consume vast volumes of text, but the point is that gaining an understanding of the IAM's Stage Model will help you get the most value from your Links Business Group LLC materials. For instance, this *Volume 1* guide is squarely targeted at *Concepting* and a bit of *Pre-planning*. Other volumes in the series will focus on stages 2 - 6, and be presented as a comprehensive *IAM Success* package.

One crucial IAM Stage generally not discussed in other publications is what we call the "Rinsing and Repeating" stage. This Stage is so crucial because IAM can never be "done." After all, do you make a sale to a valued client and say "we're done now – see you later?" No! You have to continually review, evaluate, tune, improve, tweak, configure, modify, plan, support, and concept your IAM Program. Like anything else in today's 24x7x365xGlobalxNonstop business world, IAM is always growing, evolving and improving. Tools and methodologies improve continually. As the IAM industry begins to mature, the pool of talent is growing to help organizations plan and execute successful IAM strategies. Do not miss out on this opportunity to implement a successful program yourself, because rest assured, your competitors will not.

What do we mean by "IAM Success?" And what defines success?

I like to use a simple definition here. IAM Success can be broadly categorized by the following:

✓ A program that fulfills strategic business or organizational goals for the betterment of the entire organization and for those with whom it does business

✓ A program that fulfills the mission of its charter, and all documented requirements, as established by its core stakeholders

✓ A program that justifies cost in itself and adds more value to the organization than it removes

✓ A program that does not generate negative side effects such as fiscal bleed, talent loss, competitive damage, or audit pain

NOTE: Many organizations choose to view all of their projects in success terms. However, if the organization must constantly "re-adjust milestones" to reach success definitions as described above, then the program or its related projects *cannot be considered successful.* This is why most large companies are on their 3rd or 4th attempt with an IAM Program. Again, this is not the type of "success" we are striving for.

Ok – I really do want IAM to transform my organization. Now what?

Glad you asked! You have come to the right place, so let's begin the transformation by discussing the first stage of Success Tips and Strategies. All aboard and off we go...

Tip #1 – Know Where You Are

The first step in reaching for IAM Success is to determine where you are. To recap the Six Stages of IAM, we have:

1. *Concepting & Strategizing*
2. *Planning & Organizing*
3. *Designing & Architecting*
4. *Implementing & Integrating*
5. *Maintaining & Supporting*
6. *Rinsing & Repeating*

Understanding where your organization is at any point in time is truly crucial if you are to enjoy unbridled IAM Success. To help point the way, here are some sample scenarios and their corresponding place in the IAM stages:

- ❖ IAM is not implemented at all →**Concepting**
- ❖ The board or a C-level exec has just begun an IAM initiative →**Concepting and planning**
- ❖ IAM has a program charter, some sponsors, maybe even looking at some software →**Planning**
- ❖ Tool A needs to integrate with IAM Suite →**Designing**
- ❖ Developers need a common framework to add security to their applications →**Designing**
- ❖ Software, systems, workflows, requirements are vetted and ratified →**Implementing**
- ❖ Your IAM implementation is broken. Nothing integrates, vendor is unresponsive, promises are unfulfilled →**Implementing**
- ❖ Some degree of IAM has already been implemented →**Maintaining**
- ❖ You have already spent hundreds of thousands or millions on IAM and are unsatisfied →**Rinsing & Repeating / back to Concepting**

Where is your organization within the IAM Stage Model? If you're like most, you have been through several IAM Stages one or more times with mixed results. It is quite common for organizations to attempt IAM two or three times with different vendors before attaining the right mix. Most organizations actually start IAM somewhere around Stage 3 or 4. Stage 1 is often ignored completely or glossed over, Stage 2 is not completed in depth, and by the time you reach Stage 3 you are designing something in response to an event or the recommendations of your new IAM tool vendor or auditor, rather than something that your business really needs.

Our goal here is to get your organization back to Stage 1. Regardless of how far along you are in the process, it is a fiscally and politically prudent move to revisit Stage 1 on a semi-annual basis at the least. Doing so will help ensure that your program stays on track, remains fiscally and organizationally responsible, and maintains alignment with strategic business goals.

Tip #2 – Stop Wasting Money

This is my favorite tip, and one that often brings in new clients because everyone can relate to this. Many organizations – not all, but many – have experienced multiple failures with past IAM Programs. The reasons are myriad (and discussed elsewhere,) but the point is that they have failed and lost money one or more times in the past.

> *Failure =lost opportunity, lost revenue, political damage, lost talent, lost capital.*

There are other losses and damages to be sure, but the failure of any Enterprise Initiative, whether it is Enterprise Resource Planning (ERP), IAM, Collaboration/Messaging, or Data Warehousing (and many others) equates most significantly to fiscal loss. The stakes are high, margin for error is great, and opportunity costs are substantial for either *doing IAM incorrectly or not doing IAM at all* .

Exactly how much money can be lost in a failed IAM Program? Consider these cases:

- ❖ A utility company that spent 15 million USD on four different IAM "solutions" only to end up with nothing
- ❖ A financial services company that tried three different solutions from three different vendors over the span of 7+ years without success
- ❖ A large hospital that spent three years and 2 million USD trying to implement one vendor's access management solution for patient record management. After three years, they were still working on it, and doctors were still accessing records the "old" way
- ❖ An insurance conglomerate spent over 11 million on a provisioning solution that was killed on the 11th hour, never to be heard from again
- ❖ And many, many more….

What did these organizations have in common?

- ❖ Little or no *Concepting*
- ❖ IAM Programs driven by cataclysmic organizational events (tactical responses)
- ❖ Vendors who overpromised and under delivered
- ❖ IAM implementations that were not driven by strategic business goals
- ❖ Users who saw no value or even detriment in the proposed solution
- ❖ Buggy, inconsistent software that could not be made to work without significant backline engineer support – if at all…

Isolated cases? Unfortunately, no. The stakes are high, and losses can be great for organizations not taking the time to properly concept and evaluate why IAM or any strategic initiative should be undertaken in the first place.

The tip, then, is to apply a hard stop to any IAM Program which is not fully meeting the success definition. *Stop and evaluate your past, current, and projected expenditures.* Consider spending a bit more time on *Concepting* and getting the right people to the table early, rather than on software seats and licenses.

One note before we leave this tip: a common objection to this tip is "but...we're *in* implementation right now! We are configuring software component X to interface with our internally developed component Y, and if we stop now, all these terrible things will happen!" My response to this objection is, *are you in Stage 5?* If you are, then a hard stop is not the answer. In that case, you can go back to Stage 1 and check your program against the original strategies, concepts, and project plans.

Unless you are In Stage 5, a hard program pause may well be in order. This pause (or hard stop) should be used critically to evaluate economic spend vs. projected results. I did say *economic spend* and not *capital spend*. If IAM becomes a non-strategic, strictly capital cost, bottom-line endeavor, it will never cost justify itself. Economic cost principles must be factored in to all Stages of your program.

Costing in the real world

A side bar is in order. From an IAM Program perspective, it can be safely said that most organizations, especially those of any significant size, will never accurately project capital and economic costs. Some organizations come very close, even to the point of adding or removing vast swathes of personnel and infrastructure to satisfy organizational (or Wall Street's) mandates. But by and large, politics, incomplete cost models, convoluted vendor pricing models, and bottom-line vs. economically driven management models prevent organizations from attaching true and absolute economic costs to enterprise-scale problems. This is why we emphasize *evaluation* and *reevaluation* to maintain alignment between strategic business goals, and the enterprise IAM Program. Ditto with ROI. The "new" wisdom states that no one focuses on ROI any more, at least within the IAM arena. While I believe that ignoring ROI is extreme, I will shout loudly from the rooftops that it should never be the primary focus of IAM. ROI is simply one measurement, but remember that vendors, politics, and shifting market forces will all conspire to ensure that ROI numbers remain at best approximations, and at worst, farcical subjections.

Tip #3 – Start Strategically and Don't Panic

"Joe, we were just massacred on this latest SOX audit"

"Donald....yes...I know....it's really been hurting us for the past few quarters. The organization has been pouring hundreds of thousands of dollars into auditing our systems and tracking down identity information. Every time we do this, we have to pull our key people off strategic business projects to prepare reports for the auditors."

"Joe – what can we do about this? What do the auditors recommend?"

"Well Donald – they say we need to fix our processes – and fast. We need better accountability, better auditing, a way to prove that the controls we spent time documenting are actually followed by our personnel and security systems.

"Joe, can software solve our problem?"

"Donald...sure, sure. As a matter of fact, there is a new type of auditing software that will just hook transparently into our all our systems and provide us with whatever reports we need. Just a couple of clicks, and we can cut our response time by 75%, and our audit costs by 80% with just one installation!

"Joe, let's get on that right away. Call the vendor and let's talk to purchasing."

This semi-fictional dialog between two managers is a slightly modified version of real conversations happening in today's hallways and boardrooms. There is a class of software in the IAM marketplace, which I refer to as *panicware*. The idea behind "panicware" is that a vendor rushes to market in response to some event – say, the passage of a new and obscure financial regulation, Sarbanes Oxley in the States, or any of the other myriad domestic and international regulations. As organizations panic responding to scenarios for which they are unprepared; some vendors promise speedy resolutions which are completely unobtrusive to the organization. These "unobtrusive" solutions are so smooth and wonderful, that the organization will hardly know the tool is even there. The solutions just hum silently along, solving all the problems in the background, so that organizations can continue with their status quo, or "business as usual." (NOTE: This is not intended as a blanket statement as there are some good and ethical vendors, with quality products.)

Does the preceding scenario perhaps seem a bit unrealistic? If you answered yes, then you are well on your way to implementing Tip #3, which is "Begin Strategically, not as a knee-jerk reaction or panic response to an event." All too often, true IAM Programs start from a reactive and not proactive organizational plan. Granted, ideal strategic circumstances are never really there for most organizations. As in life, responding to a drastic event late may be better than not responding at all, but it will certainly not have same outcome that a prepared organization might enjoy. The prepared organization views an audit as a check and balance, and an opportunity to test the current operation of its people, processes and systems

Don't let the panicware scenario happen to your organization. Achieving the advanced stages of IAM including universal business process, federation, re-usable data, increased user and satisfaction and the myriad of other benefits requires a strategic plan, and focus. Let's take the strategic focus on to *Tip #4 – Starting from the end.*

Tip #4 – Start from the End

Now that your organization has decided to begin strategically, the idea behind *Tip #4* is that before you even start your program and just when the discussion is forming, when goals are being reviewed, when gate-keeping entities are reviewing projects and programs and determining things that make sense for the organization to pursue - it is at this very early stage that it makes sense to look at:

❖ Where are the business goals taking you?
❖ What are the various internal and external drivers for your program?
❖ What are your primary pain points?
❖ What high-level requirements are driving you to even consider an IAM Program?
❖ What would the end state look like in the ideal world?

Now obviously, if your organization is fully deployed in an IAM Program and has re-architected business process to fit your new model, you may not have the same considerations. However, if you're just starting out or maybe you're doing an IAM restart, take a page from classic Project Management, and seek to work backwards from the end. Determine what you want your business to look like in identity terms three to five years down the road.

Now I realize that's kind of a long-term view for most organizations today, but certainly you can determine a working end state. What is an example of an end state? Examples might include:

❖ *I want help desk password resets to be reduced by 50%.*
❖ *At the end, I want to reduce my application portfolio by three, five or ten.*
❖ *At the end, I want to have universal provisioning across my portfolio of 10, 50, 100 or more applications. (500 or more is common in large organizations.)*
❖ *At the end, I want my online customers to have a consistent experience throughout all areas of my website*

The preceding end goals are just representations, but they're typical of consistent goals that organizations should be seriously looking at. Starting from the end means always planning in terms of goal and result, and letting these ends drive your program planning back toward a logical start. Don't be afraid to aim high with the higher-ordered IAM State. Don't be afraid to start with the idea that you want all of your applications to support fully externalized authentication and have the ability to audit and run detailed reports throughout your organization.

Avoid viewing the end state in terms of a rigid set of bullet points. Instead, view the end state in the context of goals and frameworks which can allow the goals to be realized. In the early stages, you don't necessarily know everything and every single result, or everything that the IAM Framework can accomplish in three or four years.

To summarize, determine the business benefit value in reducing the number of user sign-ons, adding privacy, reducing your application time to market, automation of manual tasks, adding auditing and detailed views of "who is doing what," and consistent role modeling. These are the kind of things that come from the business benefit side, and I can't emphasize enough that *when you're starting with the end in mind, the end has to be completely business driven.*

Tip #5 – Plan for a Changing Endgame

Now that your IAM end game has been planned and committed to paper or digital bits, you have to build in the "flex" to accommodate a constantly changing world, marketplace, and technology landscape. Your end game from *Tip #4 is going to change,* so you need to plan accordingly. That means building flexibility into your framework, building the right IAM Program Team early, realizing that team members will change, business needs will change, applications will change, regulatory environments will change, things in the industry will change, your competitors will change and new technologies will make things faster, better, cheaper. So as you move forward, your end game is going to change. Business today can be a rapidly moving target: *remember that you need to shoot at where the target is going, not where the target was standing yesterday.*

Inside and outside of your organization, factors such a reorganization and realignment, and technological technologies are always modifying the application landscape. Technologies such as SOA, thin client, thick client, bandwidth considerations, virtualization, any number of infrastructure initiatives also determine how you're going to implement Identity & Access Management. As the game constantly changes, keep sight on your higher order end state, but realize that the end point is going to change and be sure to plan for it. This especially means having the right team in place and also having a program plan built with some flexibility to handle dynamic scenarios.

NOTE: The "How To" discussion of specific planning activities is covered in *IAM Success Tips: Volume 2*.

Tip #6 – Use the IAM Cornerstones to Concept Your Program

IAM consists of three primary components, which we refer to as the "IAM Cornerstones"

1. *Access & Authorization*
2. *Provisioning & Management*
3. *Auditing and Reporting*

At the Concepting or early Planning Stages, it is easy to get caught up in the technology, network components, who will be managing everything, endless meetings, what your support team will look like, which vendor you will select and a myriad of other factors associated with traditional IAM Programs. They key for *Tip #6* is to define which of the three IAM cornerstones are most important to your organization, and to use that information when Concepting your program.

Here a few points of consideration:

❖ *Access & Authorization* includes directories, access methods (tokens, certificates, username/password, biometrics, etc.) SSO, eSSO, Federation, web services security and SOA-related security.

→*TIP: As a highly general rule, the reporting features of Access & Authorization tools are not comprehensive enough for most organizations. I recommend keeping Access and Authorization as a goal separate from Auditing and Reporting. (See below.)*

❖ *Provisioning* includes adding users to systems, removing users from systems, traditional systems administration tasks such as password reset, user self service, password synchronization, setting home directories, password policies, business process management, and task workflow/automation.

→*TIP: Most if not all provisioning solutions offer a degree of auditing and reporting. Depending on which products are ultimately implemented, the provisioning tool(s) may not provide detailed access or authorization auditing for all of your connected systems. This would include database management systems and host-based systems, just as two examples. This topic will be covered in greater detailed in Success Tips Volumes 3 and 4.*

❖ *Auditing and Reporting* includes auditing user access to systems (*Access & Authorizations,*) user-generated profile actions (password changes, security questions, etc.) and general "who has access to what and where did they go within the systems they have access to" questions.

→*TIP: It is common for most IAM 'suites' to have some level of auditing and reporting spread throughout their myriad software components. However, most fall short in the area of integrated reporting, which is designed to get managers and auditors the information they need, in the format in which they need it. To achieve this higher order reporting, you will eventually need to consider third party solutions, or building your own reporting system which can pull access, authorization, and provisioning information from multiple data sources.*

Using the preceding information during the Concepting Stage can make your later Planning Stage far more effective. I cannot emphasize enough that *you should not get hung up on the technology in the Concepting Stage.* The IAM software market is literally awash in quality commercial and Open Source IAM products, with more arriving daily. Selecting the best products to meet your needs will happen during the later phases of your IAM Planning Stage (More on this topic in *IAM Success Tips: Volume 2.*)

> →*TIP: Most organizations today really want detailed auditing and reporting, and/or increased end user convenience. If your organization is driven more toward one versus the other, then be sure to explore them thoroughly in your Concepting Stage. This exploration is valuable, because it gives your organization the opportunity to scale back what could potentially be a very large and expensive program, and concentrate on delivering a tighter deliverable that truly meets your needs.*

Tip #7 – Get Your Input Early

Tip #7 can be illustrated with a brief scenario. For this scenario, we will use two fictional companies: IAMHappy, LTD. and IAMSad, LTD. Though these companies are purely fictional, their stories are very much based on real-world IAM Programs. *Any similarity to real and physical companies or company names is purely coincidental.* As the company names might imply, IAMHappy sought input early, IAMSad did not. For brevity and effectiveness, we will skip all the details of each respective IAM Program, and concentrate on communications and input.

Let's look into their respective programs....

IAMHappy, LTD – Bringing people to the table early

IAMHappy, LTD is a large multinational media company. It has over 100,000 users in 40 countries. In early 2005, it decided to embark upon a massive multiyear IAM Program with price tags well into the millions for all associated products, services, infrastructure, and internal effort. IAMHappy determined that it wanted to be effective and efficient with its program, and make it highly business relevant. Early in the Concepting Stage, it identified the key stakeholders (*See Tip #10*) created a communications framework (*See Tip #9*), and began seeking required input. During the first three months of its program, all key stakeholders were identified, communications went out, bi-directional comment portals and blogs were established, and the program newsletter sent routinely.

As the communications media worked their way through the organization, much useful feedback was gained. From the technical people, database security policy issues were uncovered which would have to be addressed by any potential IAM product vendor. From one of the key media creation units, secure high-speed ftp requirements were discovered and portal developers needed a means to externalize security. Data security providers uncovered a number of requirements pertaining to user access, entitlements, and reporting. Though IAMHappy was fully aware that it could not feasibly please everyone, nor could it plan to gather every last requirement in the organization before embarking on the program, it did know that by taking the first three months to conduct interviews and uncover true stakeholders, its chances of being relevant and successful would increase exponentially.

By taking the first few months to really communicate and Concept, while assiduously following *Identity & Access Management Success Tips*, IAMHappy got its program off the ground the right way. Now let us fast forward to year 2 of IAMHappy's program. Here are a few of the results:

❖ 40% of the identified application portfolio is fully integrated to its chosen IAM Framework. A great achievement, given a portfolio of over 500 core applications.

❖ IAMHappy's key artwork supplier has now successfully completed its first Federation test. Both organizations have agreed to share a common set of identity attributes to facilitate system access, communications, reduce time to market, and increase worker productivity

❖ Employees are now able to seamlessly log in to their company portal, HR benefits pages, file shares, and email systems

❖ Managers have regained valuable person hours by not having to spend hundreds of thousands of hours combing through access and audit logs to appease outside auditors. Much of this information is already available via their online IAM Reporting System, and the systems that are not yet integrated, will be within the next six months.

❖ Database security issues which could have potentially derailed the program were caught early and addressed with the IAM vendor and the database vendor. Given that the company has literally hundreds of distributed databases, this move alone saved the company over 2 million dollars.

❖ *...And the list goes on*

Sounds pretty good doesn't it? IAMHappy has taken a measured yet assertive approach to its program, and knows that it won't get everything it wants overnight, but *can* get there in reduced time by carefully Concepting and Planning the right way from the beginning. Now let us see how IAMSad, LTD. is doing with its program...

IAMSad, LTD – Bringing people to the table late if at all

IAMSad, LTD is a large utility company. It has over 20,000 users in 10 countries. In early 2006, it determined that it had several IAM-related needs and wanted to investigate the possibility of a full scale IAM Program. Things started off very well. The company knew it had several key needs, had spent time off site determining business goals, and began with an early requirements-gathering exercise to aid the Concepting and subsequent Planning Stages. It had defined some business goals defined from which to build and had consulted with a handful of people from two different departments.

With a handful of details and some overly broad goals defined, it went to work creating models, charters, and program documents. The program stakeholders decided to let a couple of other managers in on the plan. But the two other managers didn't have much to add, and felt that such a broad program might be too risky politically, so the managers began to water down the original premise. As stakeholders were identified, the program actually contracted rather than expanded. Managers spent significant time debating minutia and scheduling many talks to agree to more talks.

Communications started out broad, but gradually reduced. Key stakeholders came to find out about the program only through indirect channels, rumor, and innuendo. Questions about the program were deflected to those politically appointed people who were deemed by other politically appointed people to be the most likely to give a politically acceptable answer. In short, communications were tightly controlled, slightly expanded, contracted, removed, reinstated, and then gradually tailored for each and every distinct audience group within the company. In other words, everyone in throughout the entire organization received a completely different picture and message as to what the program was attempting to accomplish. No two people in the organization could give the same answer as to what the IAM Program mission actually was.

Long story short, key subject matter experts, developers, helpdesk, and infrastructure managers were not brought in until after the program team had decided who would, and who would not be allowed to know the program details. The helpdesk identified some key process issues that if addressed, could save up to 2 million USD per year. Program sponsors did not want to hear this. A key developer manager committed to supporting and using program services as soon as they were available. The program sponsorship deemed this as not viable. As time went on, the list of key issues that were not being heard, discussed, or socialized, multiplied exponentially. Issues were not discovered until after expensive vendor products were purchased, and consultants brought in from the outside.

At the end of 2007, almost a full two years after IAMSad, LTD embarked on its IAM Program Concept; here is a partial progress report:

❖ Helpdesk administrators ask daily if there will ever be a user self service component to allow reduction of password resets and related tasks

❖ Vendor systems are in development and production, but only two teams use them – and even when they are used, the use is sporadic and without meaningful purpose

❖ Highly manual database security management and provisioning processes go unaddressed, though the issues have been communicated to stakeholders for almost 2 years.

Addressing these early could have made a lot of difference in the program status

❖ Some departments have gone out on their own and began counter IAM-related programs to serve their localized needs

❖ No self service is available

❖ No single sign on is available, even for two applications

❖ *...And the list goes on*

As you can see, the illustrations above are not solely dependent on *Tip #7*. The outcomes described can be affected by all of the *IAM Success Tips*, and choosing to apply or not apply them. The main take away from our semi-mythical companies, is that getting cards on the table early, and taking business and stakeholder needs seriously, is a primary key to success. There is nothing more demoralizing or expensive as getting mid way into a costly multi-year program, only to find that there are key showstoppers popping up all the time; showstoppers that could have been avoided by soliciting feedback and input early in the process.

Still need convincing?

If the above is not enough to convince you, here is a real-world list of bad things that can and do happen when the *right input is not captured and addressed early*:

1. Nothing gets started, or the *wrong things* get started.
2. Subject matter experts (SME) tune out of the process, or refuse to share key details that could bring your program to a crashing halt later down the road. Some may decide that the program is a threat to their current processes, jobs, and way

of life and either outright sabotage the program, or ignore it completely and refuse to help you.

3. Managers whom would otherwise have key stakes in the process begin to badmouth the program, or worse – decide to start their own counter programs, duplicating effort, increasing cost, wasting valuable organizational resources in the process.

4. IAM software vendors may be improperly selected. Without all the data up front, it is impossible to select the best vendor(s) to help build the program. For instance, perhaps you need a particular adapter that only one vendor has, or need a special data evaluation engine supplied by another. Without the right requirements and input up front, you may purchase the wrong product on both fronts and have to later re-evaluate (and explain to the board,) a brand new purchase.

5. Organization enters "thrash" mode by continuously churning through old processes that no longer work, or creating stop-gap tactical measures to address "emergencies."

6. Key program members leave the program and the company, or are otherwise reassigned to other, less critical tasks.

7. Hundreds of thousands or even millions of dollars are lost, never to be reclaimed.

8. End user dissatisfaction flourishes.

9. Customer and client dissatisfaction grows. Clients leave or continually bombard your client service desk with complaints and issues relating to the fact that they cannot have a single log in, or own management of their own accounts.

10. *...And the list goes on*

Don't end up like poor IAMSad, LTD. Follow the *IAM Success Tips*, get the critical input, and apply the knowledge learned.

Tip #8 – Commit to a Focused Start and Outcome

It is time to fly (a bit...) in the face of conventional wisdom. Conventional wisdom in the IAM arena states "start very small, with very specific goals, get lots and lots of acceptance and buy in, then gradually move up the scale." All in all, not bad advice for some organizations. However, let me propose an alternative. Having been deeply involved in dozens of IAM-related deployments throughout the years, I can say unequivocally that what it really comes down to is a *matter of focus.* Organizations that have started out small and with tightly scoped timelines have failed just as much if not more as larger-scale programs with much broader ambition.

Lack of focus and ambiguous scope are the real killers of enterprise programs. Size itself is not the enemy, though a word of caution is in order: size *can* lead to scope creep, staffing, and management challenges. Here is a customizable scenario that we have seen work well in most environments:

❖ Define strong requirements and requirements-driven use cases.

❖ Determine a round trip or "first release" scenario that would have strong organizational impact and net positive effects. Examples might include:

   o User self service for 2 - 3 critical applications
   o Single sign on for email/collaboration software, network file sharing, and HR application
   o Provisioning of users to and from these 2 – 3 applications

o   Bi-weekly report mailed to key managers showing things such as provisioning activities, logins, who has access to what application, and number of password changes

→*TIP: These are suggestions only. Most organizations have their own reporting requirements, or select the right mix of delivery goals based on the IAM Cornerstones*

❖ Perform Identity Modeling to create the most effective and extensible Identity Model for your organization. Be sure to include all classes of ID, such as internal users, partners, suppliers, clients, etc.

❖ Use the suggested model for a minimum of three months.

❖ As the enterprise model is released, begin working to integrate 2 – 3 critical business applications. In this context, integration may be defined as applications which consume the new access control/SSO, reporting, and directory services to externalize security functions.

❖ Continue adding applications, functions, and features in combinations that make strategic business sense for your organization

❖ Once the model is sound, tested, and organizationally supported, begin a test of Federation with a key partner or supplier.

❖ Continue growing and repeating the process over time (*IAM Stage #6 – Rinse and* repeat) until the bulk of your application portfolio has been addressed.

→*TIP: There is no hard and fast rule for determining how many applications will ultimately join your IAM Framework. A good rule of thumb is to integrate 75% of your application portfolio over a three-year period.*

To summarize, I encourage you to examine your IAM Program in the broadest possible context and really consider the above suggestions. If your organization has done its homework and in the later IAM Stages selects its partners and vendors wisely, our suggested "focused start" program can work quite well. It has the added benefit of garnering broader support within the organization and making more of a positive difference in your daily operations. Starting *too* small will have limited impact and may not even raise consciousness to the level necessary to take your program where it needs to go.

Tip #9 – Socialize IAM Plans Early, Well, and Often

This is a tip originally published quite some time ago in the Links Business Group blog. I'm going to take this opportunity to greatly expand on the original theme and emphasize its importance, along with a few suggestions and examples.

Corporate/organizational communications primer

Corporate communications is one of the most politicized areas of any organization. Often, Management, HR, and Legal – at a minimum – are involved in any communication affecting more than a few users. A broad discussion of communications philosophy and study is beyond the scope of this book, but taking the time to learn and understand some basic tenets of corporate communications can make or break the success of your IAM Program. In this section, we will cover the basics as they relate to IAM Programs, or most any enterprise initiative.

Some organizations follow the "open spigot" approach to communications, in which everything is shared with everybody. Open spigot examples may include things such as all financial data, HR program information, promotions/demotions, product betas and releases, research results, what the CEO had for dinner, and the like. An open spigot organization follows a more or less open disclosure policy to promote interaction, inclusivity, and empowerment for its staff.

On the other hand, a "closed spigot" organization tightly controls all communications. Another way to refer to "closed spigot" is "command and control." The closed spigot organization funnels all of its messages through political and silo-based filters to ensure that only some people have only some of the information, only some of the time. This communication method can lead to many negative consequences, such as subject message filtering, myth, rumor, and innuendo. The closed organization faces the most challenges to a successful IAM Program due to competing notions of what should be communicated to whom, and the occasional fear of the "one mighty senior computer user who could bring the whole program to a crashing halt with a single word of disapproval."

Note that open and closed organizations represent opposite extremes of the communications spectrum. There are many organizations that fall somewhere in the middle. I leave it to the reader to determine which model his or her organization is most closely aligned with.

Know your model, know your audience, and communicate early

Once your communications model is understood incorporate it actively in your Concepting Stage. Here is an IAM communications model that works well for many organizations:

❖ *Define stakeholders into groups.*

   Example: Group 1 = IAM Program Team, Group 2 = Senior Managers, Group 3 = Subject Matter Experts (SME's), Group 4 = Developers, Group 5 = End users, etc.

❖ *Separate out technical, managerial, company, and end-user details.*

   Each communication group will have its own information requirements. Often, we recommend that communications be combined wherever possible, with an external link provided for more in-depth, or technical information for those audience members that either require it, or are just interested from an informational perspective.

❖ *Set up a website, portal, wiki, share, blog, or other web-based mechanism for the program. Give users free and easy access.*

   It is tempting to wait until the IAM Planning Stage to set up websites, connect program information to the company portal and the like. We recommend setting up the site early in the Concepting Stage. Get the information out there early. Include the results of brainstorming sessions, strategic business goals which are driving the program, and desired end goals. This type of communication has many positive results, including increased focus, broader organizational support, and greater program alignment with other business initiatives

❖ *Start a program newsletter.*

The structure, content, and distribution method will vary widely by organization. The most important thing is to start the newsletter process early, when the program is first being Concepted. *Don't wait.* Make extensive use of hyperlinks in the newsletter to direct users to more information.

❖ *Stay away from milestone based communications during the Concepting Stage.*

This is a big one. Early in the birth of your organization, there is no need or purpose for stringent milestones. Milestones and physical deliverables will be determined and scheduled *during the IAM Planning Stage*, which will be covered in *Volume II* of our book series. Milestones and metrics can be detrimental if shared too early, and bring a lot of bad press to the program if the earliest milestones are not reached. There will be plenty of time for this later. Instead, focus the newsletter and website toward providing pure information. Include items such as:

"What is IAM?"
"What does IAM mean to our organization?"
"What do we plan to accomplish?"
"How the organization will benefit."

❖ *Determine a reasonable communications frequency.* Again, this will vary significantly by type and structure of organization, but here are some field-tested guidelines:

   o   Weekly for the IAM Program Team members
   o   Bi-weekly for mid-level and senior management
   o   Bi-weekly for subject matter experts (SME)

o Monthly for end-users

❖ *Once a communications type, structure, and frequency is determined* **stick with it.**

❖ *Leverage Web 2.0 techniques to engage managers and users in the communications process.*

Advice to "closed spigot" organizations: Open, end-user communication is coming to your shores. It may not be here today, or even next year, but *it will come.* IAM Programs are multiyear endeavors, so now is a great opportunity to consider adding Web 2.0 communication techniques. For example, start a wiki or blog for your IAM Program. Allow readers (aka your end-user base,) to post comments on the program and its goals. Provide for anonymous comments to solicit the broadest possible feedback. Appoint a program team member to moderate the comments, or rotate the duty among members.

→*Tip: Organizations frequently underestimate the amount of time and broad level of support that is required for any multi-year enterprise initiative. (But pay close attention to Tip #8...) Thus, it is best to build broad support early, and blogs and wikis offer a great opportunity to engage the audience from day one.*

Before leaving this topic, I should mention that detailed program communications plans will be developed later in the *IAM Planning Stage*. The point for now is to start building interest and momentum, and keep up with it. People can be very understanding and forgiving down the road if milestones are missed, provided that they are made to feel part of the communications process.

→*Tip: Many organizations confuse user feedback or engagement with a requirement to be input driven or consensus driven. Engaging in a dialog and soliciting feedback is good communications practice, but there should be no expectation that all users will have a direct say in the IAM Program itself. What the IAM Program does or does not ultimately do rests entirely on the agreement of its members and key stakeholders. The goal in "opening the spigot" is to build support and uncover issues that might otherwise derail the program at a later date.*

Tip #10 – Identify the Top Three Stakeholders with the Most to Win or Lose

The heart of *Tip #10* is that in any organization there are always a very small number of business drivers or agents of change. For example, the CEO may initially float the idea of an IAM Program, or perhaps a member of the technical team or application team may do so. Once the idea begins to circulate, other members of the organization may either rally to, or recoil from, the notion of a sweeping IAM Program. It all depends on the individual motivations of your key organizational stakeholders. The trick is to find out who these individuals truly are – and they may be people *other than your initial sponsor*(s) – and engage their unwavering support.

Think of enterprise programs as involving heavy doses of marketing and sales. Part of the initial Concepting Stage is to pre-sell key stakeholders on the idea of IAM. If the stakeholder feels threatened by IAM, console him or her with targeted and relevant benefits. If the stakeholder is already pre-sold, then do everything possible to get him or her to help champion the program to their constituents and partners. Viral marketing is a necessary and effective strategy for propelling positive IAM messages throughout your organization.

Finding the real stakeholders

At Links Business Group, we use the term "*RIS*" or "Real IAM Stakeholders" to refer to the true key beneficiaries of IAM at the highest levels. Another way to phrase this is that the person who sponsors, or is politically assigned to sponsor or own the program may not be the real or true beneficiary of IAM.

Here is an example. Let us say that Company X decides to embark on an IAM Program and kicks off the Concepting Stage. A C-level executive or departmental manager is 'assigned' to IAM. The manager may be affiliated with an IT infrastructure department, development team, security team, or other administrative department. What often happens is that this person may have little actual stake, or 'skin in the game' aside from owning the IAM Program, budget, and staffing. Meanwhile, executive VP's in charge of application development, operations managers in charge of data centers, or helpdesk management – all of whom have huge stakes in a positive IAM outcome – are not allowed to directly impact the program with suggestions, requirements, or budget draw. This may sound counterintuitive, but we see it all the time. IAM is assigned to "manager x" because "manager x has done this stuff before," or "manager x knows EVP y, who really likes him or her and wants him or her to have this opportunity."

Whatever the motivations, it is incumbent upon the core IAM Program team members to seek out the "RIS" within their organization, and garner their support.

Try the following stakeholder discovery questions:

- ❖ What is or will be included in the IAM Program?

- ❖ Which departments will be affected and how?

- ❖ If IAM goes well, who will benefit the most?

- ❖ If IAM runs into any glitches along the way, who will be hurt the most?

- ❖ Who will be tasked with standing in front of budgetary approval boards and asking for money or program time extensions?

- ❖ Whose job(s) will fundamentally change as the result of IAM implementation?

- ❖ Who must be trained or retrained to use the new processes?

- ❖ What technical contacts will be most needed throughout the program? DBA's? Mainframe engineers? Linux and Windows experts? Java developers? Others?

- ❖ Who outside the organization will potentially benefit the most from the IAM Program?

  →*Tip: This question is often overlooked given the tendency of IAM Programs to be introspective endeavors. However, it is vital that you factor in partners, clients, and other audiences whom may be interacting with your solutions or later request a federation contract. How might your partners benefit if you gain the ability to exchange Identity information with them? How might 3rd party consultants or contractors benefit from the ability to seamlessly log on to your various systems, or gain new remote work capabilities? How might your customers and clients benefit from the ability to log in once to your portal or order processing system, and not have to log in again to other parts of your site?*

❖ Answering these questions and applying the answers to your Conceptual Analysis will help uncover the RIS.

Remember that IAM Programs *are not the place to be political*. Politics have to stop, or at least be tempered, if IAM is to have any chance of real success within the organization. Find the RIS, garner their support in any way possible, and move forward.

Tip #11 – Appoint a Champion, an Evangelist

If you listen to Links Business Group's *Identity Management Success* Podcast regularly (http://www.linksbusinessgroup.com), you'll remember that we had quite a discussion about champions and liaisons in our *Small Business IAM* Podcast. The idea goes something like this; any successful endeavor, whether it is a revolution, great work of art, or an exciting IAM Program, *must have a champion*. Sometimes it may be one of the stakeholders identified in *Tip #10*, but most likely it will be the Program Manager, a Technical Team Member, or a manager. In smaller organizations, it is common to appoint a Security or IT Director to this role. However, and this is where we fly in the face of convention yet again, *Links Business Group LLC recommends that the IAM Program Champion **not** be a senior technical person*. Why? Because frankly, the whole point of IAM *should* be to build a program that embraces and extends strategic business goals. In large organizations, the CIO might be a natural fit for this role, as he or she is by definition, bi-located between business and technical worlds.

Champions may be selected or self appointed. Every organization is different, but here are a few tried and true attributes of a great IAM Champion:

- ❖ *Aptitude*. Capable of understanding the "big picture" and relating it to business objectives, technical objectives, and vendor service/product offerings.

- ❖ *Flexibility*. Ability to react positively to changes and the many curve balls that will be thrown by life, business, and the various stakeholders.

- ❖ *Good connections throughout the company or organization.*

- ❖ *Great communication skills.* Has the ability to synthesize both technical and business concepts to largely non-technical audiences, while clearly articulating the business cases and benefits of the program.

- ❖ *Willingness to commit long term to your program and its success*. There are no guarantees in life, and this certainly applies to staff members and employees of companies. However, it is best as a general rule to have a champion with a measured stake in your organization. Perhaps a major stockholder, long-term employee, cross-functional manager, or respected long-time technician with some strong business background. Losing a champion in the middle of the program can be disastrous, so choose as wisely as possible.

- ❖ *Organizational support, including the unimpeded ability to communicate directly with mid-level and senior managers.*

This last point is so important, that it should almost be written in bold red font. (But I won't shout….) A major cause of IAM Program Failure or "IPF," is lack of access to management. Enterprise business initiatives are the last place to build walls and create political barriers. Once again….if your organization is not committed to living the principle of unencumbered communication with key stakeholders, then do not start the program. Save your money.

Before leaving the topic, let's take a moment to review who the champion should *not* be:

❖ *The CEO.*

❖ *A consultant or contractor.*

Though it is often desirable and necessary to strategically use experienced consultants throughout your program, they should only be used for specific projects and consultative purposes. As a long-time consultant and shareholder in a company that provides consulting services, I can state without hesitation that consultants should be used for their intended purposes, and not as a full time substitute for sound organizational process. Note that I am not talking about outsourcing here, or the use of long-term specialty contractors. The point is that this crucial champion position must be deeply staked *internal* to your organization.

❖ *A nepotistic or otherwise 'politically motivated' appointment.*

Take a page from the largest software companies. Often, you will see positions or titles such as "Product Evangelist" or "Product Manager." These positions are analogous to the IAM Champion or Evangelist. Note that I took a neutral stance on the position of IAM Program Manager. It seems natural to have the Program Manager or Project

Manager act as the evangelist. There is nothing inherently wrong with this, but long-term programs have the tendency to cycle through Project Managers. They leave, get reassigned, and split duties with others as more objectives are added to the program. Even worse, they may leave for lateral opportunities within the company or leave the organization entirely. The ideal IAM Champion exists outside of that hierarchy, and focused intently on building that "rah rah" support for your IAM Program.

Tip #12 – Get Started Yesterday

"Get started yesterday" is not so much an IAM Success Tips as it is a strong suggestion or admonition. Regardless of your reasons for pursuing a comprehensive IAM Strategy – audit pain, need for better reporting, better user experience, reduced systems administration, business process improvements and all the others, the important thing is to "start yesterday." What do I mean by this? Quite simply that all organizations, regardless of size, need to be thinking and acting on IAM Strategies. Success begins with action.

Throughout this book, I have covered a lot of "start related" tips and strategies. While it may seem like overkill to do so, it is impossible to overstate the importance of starting right the first time. Here is why: in most organizations, once any type of enterprise program is started and funded, the die is cast in a singular direction. The political landscape often does not allow for later course changes, budget modifications, extensive team changes, vendor changes, and the myriad of other factors that can affect any multi-year program. That is why starting right the first time makes all the difference.

But what if we have already started our program? Is it too late?

Only your board or sponsorship team can determine whether or not it is too late. However, *it need not be too late -- ever.* The most successful IAM Programs are dynamic and fluid. Not so much so that concrete goals are never reached, but fluid enough to comfortably deal with the inevitable change that comes with any large long-term endeavor. Reviewing the program often, and communicating frequently with everyone, will dramatically reduce the chance of reaching a point of no return. When all else fails, or you need a bit of help to put the ship back on course, consider seeking a qualified outside Strategic IAM Consultant.

Conclusion – Applying the Tips + Next Steps

Congratulations! You have just learned the twelve tips of Volume 1 which are intended to target the Concepting, or pre-Planning Stage of your IAM Program. While no list of tips or hints is ever completely inclusive, I can assure you that following the tips and advice outlined above will increase your success factor many fold. Let us recap the 12 Tips:

1. *Know Where You Are*
2. *Stop Wasting Money*
3. *Start Strategically and Don't Panic*
4. *Start From The End*
5. *Plan for a Changing Endgame*
6. *Use the IAM Cornerstones to Concept Your Program*

7. *Get Your Input Early*
8. *Commit to a Focused Start and Outcome*
9. *Socialize IAM Plans Early, Well, and Often*
10. *Identify the Top Three Stakeholders With the Most to Win or Lose*
11. *Appoint a Champion, an Evangelist*
12. *Get Started Yesterday*

From discussion to application – applying the tips

Here are a few useful hints when applying the *Identity Management Success Tips*:

1. Everyone on the Concepting Team should read this book at least twice.

2. Concept in seclusion. At the Concepting Stage, a common mistake is to not send people offsite or otherwise dedicated place for brainstorming and mind mapping. *If you are serious about IAM, dedicate an initial Concept Team, and invest in putting them offsite somewhere for at least two full days.* Remove distractions such as cell phones, Blackberries, and laptops (except for the dedicated scribe.) If you are not serious enough about your IAM Program to finance this vital first step, then it is time to seriously evaluate whether or not an IAM Program is right for your organization.

3. Keep all discussions at this stage limited to thinking and talking about the IAM Program. *This is not a project planning exercise. Do not start planning your project yet.* Planning without solid Concepting and sound organizational management principles will cause your program to fail. Planning will be covered in detailed in *IAM Success Tips:*

Volume 2

4. During your offsite, bring in at least one member from each major business unit or line of business to give a ½ to 1 hour talk. The talk should cover IAM from their organizational point of view, and what goals they would like to realize.

5. Have fun. Admittedly, this can sound a bit hackneyed but your team should really strive to have some fun with IAM. It can be an exciting, challenging, and exhilarating journey when done well. The traditional old world view of IAM was something like this "it's big, ugly, and expensive." This sort of negative spin and lack of focus can really hamper enthusiasm and drive. IAM is a marathon, and not a sprint – a journey, rather than a destination, an endeavor, rather than a task. How you frame and communicate your program from the outset, can determine a failed or successful outcome.

6. Enable your portable audio device or computer headphones and listen to our *Identity Management Success Podcast Series*. (http://www.linksbusinessgroup.com)

    NOTE to Managers and C-level Executives: Links Business Group's *Identity Management Success Podcast Series* is an important and valuable medium which can provide significant useful information to your program and technical people. One way to think of it is like ongoing training that costs little to nothing for any company. Consider providing headphones to your employees and network users so that they can keep up with the latest information in *Identity Management Success* concepts and tips. Visit http://www.linksbusinessgroup.com for the latest information on our podcasting schedule and recent episodes.

What happens next?

The next step is up to you! This book has covered a lot of ground but this is just the beginning.

Additional books in this series will be released throughout 2008 and 2009. The upcoming *IAM Success Tips Volumes* will continue our journey in providing you with support, tools and strategies to achieve your ultimate goals. *IAM Success Tip: Volume 2* is slated for release in June 2008. This new volume will cover the *IAM Planning Stage in depth, and cover crucial Program Planning topics such as team selection, budgeting, selling, presenting, establishing vendor and product selection criteria, how to achieve accurate planning projects, and much, much, more.* In the meantime, please visit our companion website at http://www.linksbusinessgroup.com for our latest vendor-neutral IAM information.

In addition to the IAM, Business Consulting, and Strategic IT information posted on our website, you can:

- ❖ Listen to the *Identity Management Success Podcasts*
- ❖ Join our exclusive members-only online community and receive special discounts on all Links Business Group LLC materials in addition to many bonus items not available to the general public
- ❖ Contact Links Business Group LLC to request more information on IAM books, products, training, or to a complimentary consultation with one of our highly trained consultants.

Book my services as a public speaker and trainer today. Many organizations find this an effective way to present IAM Program Principles and Implementation Strategies to their employees and large groups of people. You can arrange for my speaking services by calling the Links Business Group LLC offices at **+1 877 769 8938**, or write to info@linksbusinessgroup.com for more information. Links Business Group is a global business entity and can meet your needs throughout the world.

Thank you all for reading!

Until next time: all the best of Identity Management Success.

Corbin H. Links, President
Links Business Group LLC

Epilogue

You are now ready to formally Concept your program and conduct the preplanning stage. As you begin your program, or restart your organizational IAM journey, remember that there are no shortcuts. There are many tips and techniques to shorten the cycle, but not to short circuit solid process building.

Carefully consider your relationship to technology. Many organizations place far too much stock in technology, and the promises it seems to bring to the table. In the early Concepting and later Planning Stages, it is very tempting for organizations to focus all their efforts on technology. For instance, a vendor makes an attractive product pitch and aggressive price proposal, and the organization immediately starts to build a concept around it. Technology is constantly changing – we've talked about that a lot. What you should also know is that there are few really 'next big things' in technology, similar to the number of available themes for a written novel. Much of IAM has grown up around the massive IT decentralization trend which followed the mainframe's fall from grace. IAM and related Strategic Enterprise Programs seek to recentralize in a matter of speaking, and bring some order out of the chaos imposed by too many systems, connected to too many things, by too many different vendors.

One last suggestion before we temporarily part ways en route to the Planning Stage. Wherever possible, please try to keep the IAM Stages rigidly separate. Good programs have fluidity, but they also have significant milestones and 'hard stop' points in which status can be disseminated, and used as metrics. *Ensure Concepting is fully complete before putting a plan to paper.* Many organizations opt to later add the time and resources used for Concepting to a project plan. Steadfastly avoid trying to populate a project management program or spreadsheet with all manner of task until the program is fully concepted. You will be glad you did!

Appendix A – Additional Stage 1 Success Articles

In the weeks following the first release of *IAM Success Tips: Volume 1*, we collected and compiled a number of select articles from the industry-leading Links Business Group LLC Blog. These supplemental articles are provided here in this expanded version of *Volume 1*. Please enjoy and benefit from this complimentary new information, while assiduously applying the knowledge to your current or future Strategic Business Initiatives.

IAM / IdM Definitions, Acronyms and Abbreviations

In this article, we explore just a few key terms used in everyday Identity and Access Management (IAM.) The terms presented are not comprehensive of all facets of IAM, but instead cover commonly used conventions common to Links Business Group LLC materials.

Access Management - The process of:

1. Determining a set of authorizations and privileges that a validated identity may have on a computing resources
2. Controlling entitlement by granting or denying access to resources

Access Manager

The portion of IAM that authorizes and control access to computing resources based on predefined or customized policies. Many IAM and especially AM, or Access Management vendors, use this term in their product names.

Adaptors / Connectors

Provide an interface between targets (systems to which access is granted or denied,) and the Access/Authorization modules within an Identity Management System -- also known as "connectors." Some IAM products recognize a difference between "Agents" which perform an action on behalf of a system and/or user, and "Adaptors" which allow a template approach for connecting from an "IdMS," or Identity Management System, to various target systems containing data, such as databases and directory services.

Auditing & Reporting

Comprehensive, enterprise-wide auditing and reporting of identity profile data, change histories, and user permissions, ensuring that security risks are detected early, allowing proactive response by administrators. The ability to review the status of all identity access privileges at any time improves audit performance and helps achieve compliance with regulatory requirements. Reporting on usage of self-service password resets and time metrics for the provisioning and de-provisioning of users provides management with high visibility into key operational metrics and operational improvements.

Authentication

The process of establishing whether an identity is valid in a particular context or system. A client may be an end user, a machine, service, or an application. If credentials provided by the client are valid, then the client is considered to be an authenticated client. It is important to note that

Authentication is simply the act of validating that an identity is active and valid within the Identity Management System. Once authenticated, the identity requires *authorization* to do meaningful work.

Authorization

The process of verifying that an authenticated client has sufficient rights and permissions to access the requested resource. Note: depending on context, "rights" are generally analogous to "Access Policies," or "Access Rules," whereas "Permissions" are analogous to Access Control Lists (ACL), or broadly stated "what an Identity is allowed to do with a particular resource." Common authorization permissions include "Read / Write / Execute / View / Print / Move / Change Ownership" and many, many others. Permission implementations *vary widely* between IAM tool and target implementations.

Authorization Decision Assertion (ADA)

Specific to SAML (Security Assertion Markup Language). An ADA is an assertion, or credential, which determines what actions an identity is able to perform.

Credentials

Physical representations of an Identity, and its related *permissions*. When using an Identity to access a resource, the *credential* must present proof the identity belongs to the person, system, or process. When credentials are presented to a security authority at the Policy Enforcement Point (PEP), the authority will authenticate the credentials, thereby validating the identity.

Directory Service

A directory service associates names and identities with objects and attributes. Depending on implementation, a directory service can encompass access, authorization, auditing, and policies, white and yellow pages. Thus, you not only can look up an object by its name but also get the object's attributes or search for the object based on its attributes. A directory service, whether standalone, federated,

Meta, or virtual, provides the backbone of an Identity Management System.

Entitlements

A set of authorized accesses that are attached to an authenticated Identity. This set of accesses may also be referred to as "grants" or "entitlement grants." Entitlements can be highly specific, and refer to applications, parts of applications such as specific web pages, or even individual functions within the application code, such as transactions. Entitlements tend to be application specific, while credentials are more generic and system specific.

Federation

A module or standalone component of an Identity Management System (IMS), which provides a "web of trust." Provides a method for business partners to mutually agree on how to authenticate and authorize users, and which users to trust. Users authenticated by one organization's Identity Management System can pass transparently to a partner business without having to re-authenticate. (A form of multi-partner single sign on.)

IAM

Identity & Access Management. Often used interchangeably with the term "IdM," depending on vendor, and context. Some vendors now use the variation of "IdA" or "Identity Access" to cover the same components.

Identity

A unique set of data, such as a token, username, fingerprint, or social security number, combined with attributes that uniquely describe an entity. The entity may be a user, an application or a service. Identities are mapped or associated with specific individuals and services, and then managed within the context of an Identity Management System. A unit of Identity uniquely identifies who and what can access the system.

A simplified view of Identity is an object, such as a user name, that is completely unique within a given system. The unique object has some number "attributes" or adjectives, that describe it. *Remember that an Identity always has one or more attributes. Without attributes, there is no Identity.*

Identity Management System (IMS / IdMS)
Comprehensive framework, typically existing within a set administrative boundary such as a domain or organization, which provides Access and Authorization Management, Auditing, Reporting, Strong Authentication, Federation, Identity Lifecycle Management, Adaptors, and Directory Services. Note that the IMS refers to the infrastructure, framework, software, servers, networks, and systems which collectively provide comprehensive Identity Services.

Identity Manager
The component of the Identity Management System that allows users, groups, roles, and entitlements to be added, modified, or removed. Specifically provides application provisioning services, and user self-service functions such as password changes and resets. Simply stated, the Identity Manager is generally analogous to a "provisioning system."

IdM
Industry-standard acronym which stands for "Identity Management." The terms "IAM" and "IdM" are often used interchangeably, though "IAM" is more descriptive in that it includes external access controls, in addition to identity lifecycle management.

Infrastructure
Composite combination of physical systems, networks, applications, and operating systems which provide the plumbing for IAM.
LDAP

Lightweight Directory Access Protocol. LDAP takes the "lightweight" in its name from the fact that is essentially a trimmed down version of the X.500 directory standard. LDAP is both a directory service (implemented as a physical database and related services,) and a protocol which defines the means of accessing the LDAP store. LDAP is used for yellow/white pages, authentication, authorization, and "grouping" services.

Meta Directory

Collection of directory information from various, diverse directory sources that is aggregated to provide a single, unified view of data. Meta directories often uni or bi-directionally synchronize identity and classification data with multiple directories, building the master "book of record" which can be used by people, systems, and services. Meta directories are often used as the transitional step toward a single, unified, directory store of information. One of the key differences between Meta Directories and virtual directories are that Meta Directories store and synchronize data between multiple different directories, whereas virtual directories do not store data. See "Virtual Directory" definition below.

Policy Decision Point (PDP)

The service with an Identity Management System that makes policy-based decisions, such as what user can access which resources, at which times of the day. The PDP answers queries from the PEP, and returns 'decisions' back to the PEP.

Policy Enforcement Point (PEP)

Asks or interrogates the Policy Decision Point (PDP) if the user, service, or requested operation has access and permission to perform an action. Example, can user "jdoe" access file "12345.doc" The PEP allows or disallows the user action based on the PDP decision.

Privacy

State or degree to which an Identity or part of an Identity is shared, hidden, or obfuscated from other identities, or non-identity holders.

Trust

A determination of a system or service to authenticate or authorize a "foreign" (an authentication/authorization request initiating from outside the organization's native Identity System) identity or service. In the Identity Management context, trust often refers to federated entities, which have agreements on which entities to trust (authenticate) or deny.

User Provisioning

The function of an Identity Management System that creates identities in target systems, and removes identities from the targets when no longer needed. Provisioning refers both to the service delivered by an Identity Management System, and the action of creating, adding, or removing an identity.

Virtual Directory

Similar in concept to a Meta Directory in which both directories create a single directory view from multiple independent directories — such as Active Directory, LDAP, and relational databases. However, a virtual directory is fundamentally different, in that it does not store data internally. Meta directories maintain their own data storage unit, such as a database, while the virtual directory collects and caches information dynamically.

X.500

The "father" of LDAP and the original suite of directory services protocols and standards. X.500 comprises a broad set of services which include name resolution, directory access protocols (DAP), query resolvers, schemas, naming mechanisms, and physical storage structures. In real-world implementations, X.500 became cumbersome over time, providing a monolithic directory view, placing heavy loads on the clients, and pure OSI-based protocols over TCP. X.500 and has been mostly replaced with the newer LDAP.

Top 16 Reasons for IdM / IAM

1. Significant operational cost reduction
2. Reduced time to market
3. Reduced complexity
4. Improved Service Level Agreements (SLA)
5. Improved end-user experience
6. Reduced burden of compliance
7. Unified security reporting
8. Unified security auditing
9. Improved partner integration (Federation)
10. Improved user and systems management
11. Improved application and infrastructure security
12. Reduced risk exposure
13. One step closer to SOA
14. "Future Proofing" the application infrastructure and organization
15. Embrace and extend existing infrastructure and internal expertise
16. Enables an application security subscription model

The preceding list is by no means exhaustive, and individual organizations may have additional reasons.

Remember: Fundamentally, IAM is a set of processes and policies, which are designed implemented, and managed by people. IAM is *not* a set of tools or software.

Key Regulations Affecting Identity Access Management

Introduction

In recent years, the market share of the software products and other services offered by IT companies has grown significantly, and Europe and North America saw a necessity of introducing a series of laws, regulations and standards to increase companies' data security. It is one thing to draw up the acts and introduce regulations, and it is quite another to control or dictate the implementation of these regulations. It is here where Identity Access Management Programs can help. Providing the appropriate tools, process models and checklists, Identity Access Management helps to administer user-specific security settings and policies on a cross-platform basis.

This article presents a list of major world's regulations and standards, discusses the key regulations affecting Identity Access Management, including a primary focus on the Gramm-Leach-Bliley Act (*GLB*) and *HIPAA*, and explains how IAM Programs can assist organizations to comply with these regulations and others.

Disclaimer: Privacy and Data Security Regulations are continually debated and changed, while new ones are continually enacted by world governments. As such, the subject matter is vast and complex, and our intent is to provide a survey-level coverage of key international regulations affecting IAM Programs. Links Business Group LLC is a full service, vendor neutral IAM solutions provider, but not a law firm. Links Business Group LLC provides no explicit or implicit legal advice regarding the subjects covered in this article. Additionally, the regulations and standards covered in this article are not intended to be comprehensive in scope or content.

Major Data Security Regulations and Standards

One can differentiate between UK, EU and US major laws and regulations.

UK regulations and standards:

- *Data Protection Act 1998*
- *Enterprise Act 2002*
- *Electronic Communications Act 2000*
- *BS7799-2:2002 (BS 7799) Information Security Management System. Also global standard ISO17799 (ISO 17799)*
- *BS10181 (BS 10181) Authentication and Access Control. Also global standard ISO10181 (ISO 10181)*
- *Freedom of Information Act 2000*

EU regulations and standards:

- *The Privacy and Electronic Communications (EC Directive) Regulations 2003*
- *Human Rights Act 1998*
- *Basel II Capital Accord*

US regulations and standards:

- *HIPAA - Health Insurance Portability and Accountability Act 1996*
- *Gramm-Leach-Bliley ACT aka GLB. Officially titled the "Financial Services Modernization Act of 1999"* repealed the Glass-Steagall Act opening up competition among banks, securities companies and insurance companies.
- *Sarbanes-Oxley Act aka SOX Act.* Officially titled the "Public Company Accounting Reform and Investor Protection Act of 2002", signed into law on 30 July 2002
- *SEC & NASDAQ regulations* - including SEC 17a-3, the requirement to make records, and SEC 17a-4, the requirement to keep records are most relevant.

- *PATRIOT Act aka USAPA* is the official title is "Uniting and Strengthening America by Providing Appropriate Tools Required to Intercept and Obstruct Terrorism (USA PATRIOT) Act of 2001."
- *HL7* is a standard for the healthcare industry.

Why Have Regulations at all?

Before scrutinizing some of the major regulations, let's delve into the reasons why they are so necessary. On thorough analysis, we can make a conclusion that the regulations seek to perform three main functions including:

1) Protecting the confidentiality of financial and business data.

2) Protecting the confidentiality of personal data.

3) Minimizing possible credit and operative business risks for companies.

Follow-up: the Functions of the Basic Laws

GLB (Graham Leach Bliley) and *SOX* (Sarbanes-Oxley Act of 2002) have been introduced as primary tools of investor protection, seeking to ensure the confidentiality and reliability of *financial business data*. With regard to the personal confidentiality, regulations such as *HIPAA* (the Health Insurance Portability and Accountability Act), for example, regulates the confidentiality of patient data and patients' right to view and correct personal information. (From a business vertical perspective, *GLB* is focused toward Financial Institutions, while *HIPAA* covers medical institutions and their related practices.)

The *Basel II Capital Accord* has been designed to minimize credit and operative business risks for companies. The co-founder of the law is the European banking supervisory organization, which makes financial institutions assess possible business risks.

The major goal of the *HIPAA* (Healthcare Insurance Portability and Accountability Act) regulations is to ensure the privacy of any protected health information (PHI) collected, processed, and transmitted between healthcare organizations.

Graham Leach Bliley (GLB) Act

The *Graham Leach Bliley Act*, also known as the *Financial Services Modernization Act of 1999*, has been introduced to provide limited privacy protections against the sale of private financial information (for example, bank balances, account numbers etc.) Additionally, the *GLBA* stipulates protections against obtaining personal information through false pretenses. Briefly, the *GLBA* makes financial institutions take ownership of protecting the privacy of their customers, including their nonpublic information. With this respect, *GLBA* compliance is mandatory for all financial institutions, which should (theoretically) guarantee that the information will be protected from any threat from the point of view of security and data integrity. According to the *GLB*:

1) Financial institutions including banks, insurance- or brokerage companies must securely store personal financial data;

2) They must warn an individual of their policies on sharing personal information;

3) They must give their clients an opportunity to consider whether any sharing of personal financial information.

GLB includes three major components put into place to govern the collection, disclosure, and protection of consumers' nonpublic personal information:

- Financial Privacy Rule
- Safeguards Rule
- Pretexting Protection

Financial Privacy Rule

Subtitle A: Disclosure of Nonpublic Personal Information, codified at 15 U.S.C 6801 through 15 U.S.C. 6809

The Financial Privacy Rule requires financial institutions to provide each consumer with a privacy notice at the time the consumer relationship is established and annually thereafter. The privacy notice must explain the information collected about the consumer, where that information is shared, how that information is used, and how that information is protected. The notice must also identify the consumer's right to opt-out of the information being shared with unaffiliated parties per the Fair Credit Reporting Act. Should the privacy policy change at any point in time, the consumer must be notified again for acceptance.

Each time the privacy notice is re-established, the consumer has the right to opt-out again. The unaffiliated parties receiving the nonpublic information are held to the acceptance terms of the consumer under the original relationship agreement. In summary, the financial privacy rule provides for a privacy policy agreement between the company and the consumer pertaining to the protection of the consumer's personal nonpublic information.

Safeguards Rule

Subtitle A: Disclosure of Nonpublic Personal Information, codified at 15 U.S.C 6801 through 15 U.S.C. 6809

The Safeguards Rule, enforced by the Federal Trade Commission, requires financial institutions to have a security plan to protect the confidentiality and integrity of personal consumer information. The Rule has placed a burden of responsibility on many financial institutions with regard to 4 basic requirements:

1) Who can access sensitive customer data?

2) How are these users authenticated?

3) Are these users held accountable for their actions?

4) What can they see and modify?

This is where the classic IAM infrastructure comes in useful - Authentication, Authorization and Audit (AAA.) However, as the present-day tendency shows, this architecture, which has been used for years, is not enough in and of itself. Lots of security problems occur with orphaned accounts, weak passwords, vulnerable caller authentication at the help desk, dormant accounts, and stale or excess privileges. On the other hand, it does not mean that these weaknesses have come into existence because of some gaps in the AAA (Access, Authorization, and Auditing) technology. It is business processes and policies for managing data that have to be modified before any technology solution can be of benefit.

Pretexting Protection

(Subtitle B: Fraudulent Access to Financial Information, codified at 15 U.S.C. 6821 through 15 U.S.C. 6827)

The *GLBA* prevents somebody else's pretexing, or illegally gaining access to sensitive non-public financial information by making financial institutions take all the necessary precautions to protect and defend the consumer and their data.

Problems with the GLBA

The first problem connected with the *GLBA* is that it does not fully protect a consumer's ownership of his or her data. For example, if the customer did not directly specify that a particular piece of information cannot be disclosed, the company technically still has the right to disclose this information. Although the *GLBA* may be better than nothing, it still places a heavy onus of information management on the consumer.

Second, it is assumed that according to the *GLBA*, a company should clearly explain a complex set of legal definitions and the numerous exceptions to the law. However, such explanations can be confusing and suffer from "small print overlook." While *GLBA* notices do in fact inform consumers that their personal information will be shared, they may obfuscate who and which entities may receive the information, and what the receiving entities may in turn do with said information. A classic example of this is the dozens or even hundreds of "affiliates" which may be intertwined with some financial institutions. The affiliate organizations may be entitled to receive information as part of the "sharing" program, but their own privacy and protection measures may not be known to, or shared with the consumer.

Another key weakness is the *GLBA's* weak enforcement and compensation mechanisms, which cannot ensure compliance with even existing privacy legislation. Enforcement rests solely with federal government agencies, and their willingness or resource availability to pursue action. Presumably, the key driver toward *GLBA* within many financial institutions is the desire to keep their companies out of the front pages for privacy breach.

Possible Changes into the GLBA

Numerous change proposals include:

1) Using "opt-in" instead of "opt-out." Opt-in policies can explicitly allow a financial institution the ability to share data; however the customer must expressly check a box or sign a statement giving this authority to the institution. Without an opt-in, financial institutions can be under express obligation not to share the information provided. Essentially, the burden of information protection passes to the financial institution with "opt-in." This approach has been proposed, partially because of the practice of many financial institutions and web sites in general to automatically check the box of the "please share my information with whomever you feel like it and spam me mercilessly." This technique is how many firms get around "opt-in" by essentially opting individuals in automatically.

2) If opt-outs are still used, then financial institutions should be required to provide easy access to privacy policies at branch offices and on the Web.

3) Provide consumers with the right to review any disclosed information or to correct inaccurate or incomplete data.

4) Give states additional jurisdiction to enforce *GLBA* provisions to enhance enforcement efforts.

5) Providing clear and human-understandable privacy policies, which clearly spell everything out, and allow people to understand explicitly how their information may be used

What are some penalties for violating *GLBA*?

Violation of the *GLBA* may result in a civil action brought by the United States Attorney General, and can carry the following penalties:

1) "the financial institution shall be subject to a civil penalty of not more than $100,000 for each such violation"

2) "the officers and directors of the financial institution shall be subject to, and shall be personally liable for, a civil penalty of not more than $10,000 for each such violation."

Short Summary

The *GLBA* is certainly a step forward on the way to protect the user's financial and personal information. Identity Access Management solutions are crucial when it comes to implementing compliance automation.

HIPAA (Healthcare Insurance Portability and Accountability Act)

HIPAA is one of the most important of the security regulations imposed on many industries and companies. In some ways, it might be helpful to think of the *HIPAA* as the health industry's equivalent of *GLBA* – or vice versa. Both Acts seek to regulate the disclosure and transfer of private information; however the *HIPAA* goes much farther. A major goal of the *HIPAA* regulations is to ensure the privacy of any protected health information (PHI) that is collected, processed, and passed among healthcare organizations. This includes individual doctors, hospitals, and insurance companies.

In general, *HIPAA* can be much more complex to implement from a policy and process perspective. Considerations such as the protection of the intrinsic data itself, the physical transmission of the data, the receiving of the data, and access to the data (among other factors) must be carefully considered and planned.

How IAM Systems can facilitate compliance and security policy

Cross-platform Identity Access Management solutions are crucial when it comes to understanding risk, improving information security levels, facilitating user management and implementing role or purpose-based access controls.

Before we delve into some of the ways IAM Systems can help organizations and enterprises initiate compliance and control measures, an editorial note is warranted. *Most regulations have little if anything to do with IT, despite what most vendors would have you believe.* As you'll notice in reading through our survey coverage, laws and regulations are concerned with the *process* and *result* of compliance-related activities, not technology implementations. So for

instance, if your company kept all records on paper or in ledger books, the compliance regulations would apply just as much as they do in the 100% digitized organization. We feel this point is worthy of mention, because there is often a tendency for organizations to seek partial or full solutions to business problems solely from technology.

That said; let's look at a few ways IAM Solutions can benefit the typical organization:

1) *Protection of vital business data*

IAM solutions enable the correct assignment of rights for all IT platforms according to users' needs. Thanks to provisioning rules, and "purpose" or "needs-based information management," user accounts and authorizations can be automatically created, managed, and consequently removed in accordance with organizational or legal policy.

2) *Traceable Administration*

Logging features provide a tracking mechanism for all administration tasks and approval steps. IAM Systems, allow organizations to correlate their central Identity sources and ensure that administration tasks are performed in accordance with established policy, and not outside the system. For instance, administrators must create and manage users within the context of the IAM Platform, rather than "going local" and creating rogue accounts on native managed systems that cannot be tracked by the IAM Platform.

3) *Auditing authorizations*

Reduction of risks connected with authorization. Ensuring that only users that are both authenticated (identity verified) and authorized (expressly allowed to perform a certain action) are allowed to perform tasks.

4) *Correction of defects*

Detailed reporting and audit mechanisms allow weaknesses or defects in current security policies or system configurations to be detected and corrected quickly.

5) Creation of identities, and the assignment of identities to roles and privileges.

The IAM System provides a user-friendly interface for end-users and administrators alike provides a centralized management platforms for most if not all systems in the organization. Examples include UNIX, mainframe applications, and databases.

Conclusion

Several conclusions may be drawn from the material here. First, government agencies are becoming increasingly interested in "helping" organizations take serious stewardship of the data entrusted to them. Our company position is that organizations have a fundamental accountability to anyone who trusts them enough to share personal information, monies, or securities. Strong Data and Information Security practices make good business sense, and go a long way to establishing a bedrock of trust on which lifelong customer relationships may be built.

Second, business process and regulations in and of themselves are not enough. The newest generation of IAM Solutions can pick up where policy and process leave off and provide a mechanism for achieving — and maintaining — compliance with both current and future legislation. Though no one has a 100% crystal ball, it seems highly likely that regulations will continue to increase in number in scope. Building a strong foundation of business process and a next-generation security platform on which to implement the processes, can help future proof your organization and enable proactive responses to an ever-changing international business climate.

Identity and Privacy Regulations in the EU

Privacy regulations and how to address them are a critical component of global IAM Programs. This article provides a brief survey of various privacy regulations throughout the world.

Disclaimer: Privacy Regulations are continually debated and changed. The subject is vast and complex, and our intent is to provide survey coverage from an IAM perspective. Links Business Group LLC is a full service, vendor neutral IAM solutions provider, but not a law firm.

Links Business Group LLC provides no explicit or implicit legal advice regarding the subjects covered in this article.

The pervasiveness and power of today's Information technologies has lead to the acute necessity of protecting the citizens' privacy from third party invasion and abuse. It is more than clear that one of the demands of the global information society is the demand for autonomy and control over one's personal information. Governments respond to this privacy and protection need with a range of standards and regulations. In previous articles, we discussed privacy issues from various perspectives. Now, we will take a broader approach with special focus on the European Union's *Directive on Privacy*.

A Quick Tour of PRIVACY around the World

Before kicking off the main point of our article, it is interesting to investigate what is being done about privacy around the world.

Country	Privacy Measures
UK	Distribution of identification cards with biometric components to combat fraud and protect personal privacy.
Japan	Law enforcement notifying an individual when electronic information is stolen.
Canada	Introduction of laws and regulations to protect business and medical records.
The Netherlands	Law enforcement can obtain information without a warrant.
Sweden	A personal identification number is

	issued to every citizen by Church of Sweden, but it is not used for any legal purposes. For example, personal addresses are updated in a registry, but the personal ID number is never used on any legal document.

Even with the recent introductions of regulations and initiatives, many problems still exist. Whether or not countries belong to the EU, each country tries to search out possible ways of maintaining information privacy by enacting laws and regulations. The British government, for example, is working on the introduction of the first national identification card with biometric data embedded. The system of registry will allow government officials to track down foreign visitors on the same principle as the Homeland Security Department's U.S. Visitor and Immigrant Status Indicator Technology program.

The Canadian government is following the US and EU law enforcement example in terms of privacy laws. Since Canada has a well-developed banking network, it cannot afford the luxury of drawing up weaker laws, because doing so could result in huge financial losses in future, not to mention the legal and public loss of confidence ramifications. It is true that Canada has many privacy laws, including protection of health-related and business data. However, in past years, there have been noticed threats to data privacy.

Recently, Sweden has taken an unusual approach to addressing these concerns by involving the Church of Sweden. The Church will assign a unique personal identification number to every newly born Swedish citizen. The feature of this approach is that the personal IDs are never used in any legal documents. Instead, citizens get separate IDs from each government agency. With the development of online services, Swedish officials concluded that a Single Sign On (SSO) approach was undesirable, and thus wanted people to use different passwords for each online government function. Thus, every agency will gain more control over when, how and why a person's information has been handed out.

Identity and Privacy Regulations in the EU

Identity theft is an increasing problem within in the European Union, gradually becoming a lucrative business for organized crime on an international scale. In 1995, European countries agreed to unite all their privacy regulations that they had been elaborating for years, into one single policy: the *EU Data Privacy Directive*. As a result, the EU has a framework of standardized data-protection policies, which define cross-frontier flows of personal information and help control data protection among member states. The main goal of the Directive is to forbid the transfer of personal data to countries that do not offer the EU's acceptable levels of privacy protection.

Personal information under the directive includes name, address, telephone number, ethnic origin, religious or philosophical beliefs, political opinions, trade union membership, health information, and sexual orientation. This directive applies to any company holding personally

identifiable information, including employee information being part of HR information databases. The cases of accidental or unlawful destruction, accidental loss, alteration, unauthorized disclosure of the information should be reduced or eliminated.

How Personal Information Must be Handled (Per the Directive)

- Personal information as defined in the directive, can only be processed in cases where the subject has given explicit permission

- Nontransferable to third parties without a clear consent
- Collected for specified and legitimate purposes only
- Nontransferable to countries that lack adequate privacy protection levels
- Erased, or updated for accuracy with permission
- Protected by a corporate data controller

The EU Data Privacy Directive: Policies

- Authorities of each country-member are responsible for enforcing data-protection laws.
- The policies concern all information types, including financial, health, insurance etc.
- Since privacy is a fundamental human right, people are empowered to control the implementation and disclosure of their personal information.
- According to the legislation in some EU countries, telephone operators and Internet service providers are obliged to retain data for at least 12 months with the purpose of helping law enforcement investigations. In other countries, the retention of data beyond a limited time is forbidden.
- Personal data can be transferred to other countries provided that those countries offer adequate privacy protections.
- The information can be used for other purposes only with the individual's permission.
- The principles of data protection should apply to any information concerning an individual.
- Companies, which were caught misusing personal data might be faced with fines or public reprimands.
- The EU directive is not intended to change existing procedures and practices that member states have lawfully implemented for national security, law and order, or prevention, detection, investigation and prosecution of criminal offenses.

- Data-protection laws cover the collection, use and disclosure of information, no matter what technology has been used to collect it.

IAM in the EU

In order to comply with the European Union's Directive in Privacy, organizations can implement and integrate proper technical solutions and appropriate organizational measures. On the one hand, companies have already started to gradually introduce IAM technologies as a part of an end-to-end security solution addressing the growing demand for access control, secure authentication, and user management. On the other hand, the process of implementing IAM solutions and privacy-enhancing technologies is moving at a very low pace because of unclear incentives for companies to develop them and a lack of consumer awareness. Over time, introduction of new data privacy regulations, toughening penal measures, data breach publicity, and increased organizational awareness of IAM benefits will serve as stronger drivers for enterprises to integrate proper privacy features into information systems.

Conclusion

Analysis of the worldwide information security situation shows that all developed countries, including the EU member states, the US and the UK have data and privacy protection high on the agenda. European regulations are likely to force multinational enterprises to adopt strict, audited, data protection practices. These laws will also affect organizations and small businesses that may not consider themselves as multinational, and oblige them toward compliance. Besides, it is also critical to increase consumer and organizational awareness of Identity Management technologies, which can provide a good basis for addressing the problem of Identity theft, unauthorized access and unsanctioned use of personal data.

Of Tactics and Strategies

Today's topic explores risk, response, and planning considerations. Within the Identity Access Management Realm, organizations often take tactical responses to new business challenges. Common reasons include compliance, cost avoidance, cost reduction, audit demerits, partner/supplier pressure, and incident response. When taken individually, these reasons may necessitate tactical responses to strategic business issues. For instance, a new regulation imposed in one country of operation, may necessitate rapid application changes to support data privacy/isolation, or a custom encryption method for transporting data in the base country of operation. Consider the following "What if" scenarios from an organizational perspective. How would your organization respond? Would the tendency be toward a reflex action, or a strategic, board-level change of direction?

What if..........

- A key laptop was stolen from an HR Director, Senior Systems Administrator, or Broker?
- The EU poses a new regulation that affects storage and communication of user data?
- The SEC poses a new regulation that affects transaction tracking?
- The organization has hundreds or thousands of disparate servers, platforms, and applications that are managed individually, including user accounts?
- An outside auditor penalizes a company for improper transaction record retention?
- An outside auditor penalizes a company for inadequate separation of duties?

- One or more authentication / authorization systems become unavailable?
- Senior-level members of an organization are tired of remembering so many passwords?
- An organization had to spend hundreds of thousands of person-hours extracting, collating, formatting, and delivering audit and transaction reports?
- Your helpdesk spends 70% of its collective day managing passwords, group membership information, and general user profile data?

The list could go on, but the very real client scenarios above (and many, many, others) have driven tactical (i.e. "let's run out and buy something that will fix the problem") responses, strategic (i.e. "let's consider the problem, how it affects, what are the root causal factors, how we can best leverage our existing people, assets, and partnerships to ensure that the problem is not only addressed, but that the organization is equipped to deal with future problems — aka 'future proofing' "), or hybrid (i.e. "let's address this one problem quickly, while ensuring that the temporary measure aligns closely with the longer-term strategic direction.)

There is no "one size fits all" answer to the aforementioned scenarios. Organizations are unique, even within well-defined industry verticals; each having its own culture, business, and political considerations. As it said at Delphi: know thyself. The same holds true for organizations considering Identity Access Management Programs, ERP Solutions, Portfolio Management, or other Strategic IT Initiatives. It is crucial that organizations invest in their own cultural understanding, and ascertain how to effectively and holistically respond to real-world "what if" scenarios. From the Links Business Group, LLC perspective, the optimum state is the tactical-strategic hybrid approach. Before listing the benefits, it is important to mention that a successful hybrid approach requires a strategic foundation (people, policy, process) to be properly created, documented, and communicated to internal and external stakeholders.

Key benefits of the hybrid approach

- Reduced time to market
- Process and development re-use
- Ease of integration with both legacy and future-state applications
- Future-proofing
- Reduced maintenance

Two examples of hybrid IAM Solutions

- Use of Virtual Directory technologies to collate, centralize, re-design, and re-purpose existing repositories of Identity. A tactical organization would build a Virtual Directory and just leave it there. The agile hybrid organization would take the opportunity to build a flexible, standards-compliant directory service that is modeled and deployed in the Virtual Directory while building a new centralized directory that will serve as the enterprise "book of record."
- Use of provisioning technologies to centralize the management and reporting function. When properly implemented, enterprise provisioning tools provide a scalable way to gain administrative control over large numbers of disparate resources, within a relatively short period of time. The tactical organization would just deploy some basic provisioning and forget it. The hybrid organization leverages the data for reporting, audit baselining, and workflow automation, while working behind the scenes to centralize applications into an enterprise LDAP directory service. The strategic direction for such an organization would be to push all applications and platforms to "externalize" (i.e. use a

means outside themselves) authentication and authorization functions. As applications gradually externalize, the number of "target" systems, or systems that must be uniquely maintained for Identity Provisioning are reduced.

Conclusion

In summary, always strive to keep your organization forward-thinking when considering new purchases, programs, projects, or custom development. Apply the same litmus test to vendors as you would apply to any internal build/buy decisions. Ensure that vendors and products always conform to your strategic direction — or at least be willing to change as needed to meet your requirements. Ensure that new products under consideration will not introduce significant management overhead, cost, or support requirements solely to address a short-term tactical need. Application infrastructures that require significant support infrastructure must be capable of delivering real and measurable ROI to the organization, while addressing key strategic initiatives.

About The Author

My name is Corbin H. Links, and I am the President of Links Business Group LLC. My "formal" Strategic IT career began late in 1990, after spending several years managing contract security companies and various management roles throughout several industries. Since 1990, I have been engaged in dozens of enterprise business projects, including systems integration, software development, systems automation, network, data center, Identity and Access Management, data security, Project Management, Business Development, and a number of other projects. Prior to working as a Strategic Business and IT Consultant, I was the senior manager for a contract security company and served in other management roles across several industries including retail and records management.

Today, I am an active writer, speaker, lecturer, Business and IAM Consultant. Many of you may also know me from my work with the Links Business Group blog and podcast series.

About Links Business Group LLC

Links Business Group LLC is an international business consultancy committed to the growth and success of its clients. As a consultancy, we advise clients on how best to integrate our "PRP Principles" to gain real business value from IAM, and other enterprise programs and systems. As a product company, we provide the books, tools, and software to facilitate rapid, but thorough and successful implementation of IAM and other Strategic Business Initiatives. And as a training company, we provide courseware, classes, and materials specifically designed to create and manage Strategic IT initiatives such as Identity & Access Management (IAM) and Business Process Management (BPM).

For additional biographical or company information, please call us today at **+1 877 769 8938**, or visit us on the web at http://www.linksbusinessgroup.com.

What Others Are Saying

"Corbin Links is definitely one of the premier experts in the identity world. After years in the industry, you can sift between the individuals who just understand the components of a technology and those who truly understand its value to the business - Corbin not only has technical foresight but understands its relationship to resolving business problems as well. He brings a wealth of experience, insight and professionalism to the table, and is definitely someone you would want in your network."

Ashraf Motiwala, Director of Identity Management, Identropy, Inc.

"Corbin Links really has an uncanny ability to extract and clarify the business impact of Identity and Access Management solutions. He is one of our industry's foremost writers on the topic of real-world IAM technology solutions and has the battle scars to provide real insight into how-to-implement and where to look for pitfalls and obstacles throughout the process."

Matt Flynn, Security Architect, NetVision

"Mr. Links' professionalism as seen in his ability to balance the needs of client stakeholders with the time and budget constraints of the project ensured a successful implementation."

Dave Wessels, Project Manager, Crescent Enterprise Solutions

"Links Business Group's ability to jump in feet first and help us resolve a number of security and e-Commerce issues saved us thousands in potentially lost orders. Thanks to Corbin Links and the team at Links

Business Group LLC, we were able to get back on track quickly and fulfill more orders than ever before."

Theodore Pehnec, President, Pehnec Gems.

Made in the USA
Charleston, SC
03 January 2010